Amazon Echo

Ultimate 2017 User Guide and Manual For Amazon Echo - Everything You Need To Know

Matthews M. Rothschild

The information in the following pages is broadly considered to be a truthful and accurate account of facts, and as such any inattention, use or misuse of the information in question by the reader will render any resulting actions solely under their purview. There are no scenarios in which the publisher or the original author of this work can be in any fashion deemed liable for any hardship or damages that may befall them after undertaking information described herein.

Additionally, the information in the following pages is intended only for informational purposes and should thus be thought of as universal. As befitting its nature, it is presented without assurance regarding its prolonged validity or interim quality. Trademarks that are mentioned are done without written consent and can in no way be considered an endorsement from the trademark holder.

Table of Contents

Introduction

Congratulations on downloading this book and thank you for doing so.

The following chapters will discuss Amazon, the Echo device and how it all came to be.

There are plenty of books on this subject on the market, thanks again for choosing this one! Every effort was made to ensure it is full of as much useful information as possible, please enjoy!

Chapter 1: All About Amazon

As one of the largest retailers in the world and a company that caters to millions of different tastes, Amazon has come to be one of most known companies in the world. The company has worked hard to get where they are at but where, exactly, did Amazon come from?

Amazon was originally only a bookstore. It has its roots in books, and that shows with the majority of the Amazon-branded products. There is a lot of book-related aspects in the Amazon world, and it shows through the way that they do business. While Amazon originally sold books, they have expanded into so much more than that. Starting with DVDs and ending up with their very own cloud device, Echo, Amazon has come a long way from the original bookstore that they were in 1994.

The company, which was started in Seattle, was supposed to be a place for book lovers and people to come together. Nearly anyone could access the site, and they could purchase or sell the books that they wanted or had to get rid of. This was the main point of Amazon – to be somewhat of a marketplace for people who had booked. It also worked well for college students who needed a place to dispose of their books or to get used books for much cheaper than what they would find them in their college bookstore.

When the company began to expand to DVDs, CDs, and other items, they saw that they were going to be very popular. They began thinking of branching into nearly every other category imaginable. This was something that was important for the company and an area that they saw they were going to be able to make a lot of money from.

Not only does Amazon now sell nearly everything under the sun through their vast array of buyers and sellers but they also have their own branded items for sale. Their most popular options are their Kindle, which is a portable reading device that allows readers to choose from thousands of books in their store; and, their Echo. The Echo device works as somewhat of a directory. You can allow your Echo to find things for you, play songs that are on Amazon and even turn the lights on in your home if they are hooked up to the cloud. The Echo is one of the latest innovations from Amazon, and it has proven to be their best venture yet. This has been a great addition to the Amazon lineup and has far surpassed many of the other things that Amazon has to offer their clients and the people who are on their website.

Amazon has not only made a name for itself in the online world but as a retailer in general. Despite the fact that they are an online only retailer and they do not have any physical stores in their arsenal, they have become the number one retailer in the United States, passing over even some of the biggest brands that have held that spot for decades.

Since Amazon has grown so much as a company, many people have wondered how they make their money. There are three major ways that the Amazon megabrand makes their money and they have worked hard to make sure that all three of these ways have made them money.

When Amazon first started, they used their ability as the middleman to make money. People who wanted to sell had to pay a percentage of their total selling price to Amazon. This was not a lot of money out of the amount that the seller would make but, with so many people selling on Amazon, it built up a lot of money for the company. The sellers were the ones who funded it and buyers rarely had to pay any type of fee. If they did, it was because the seller had already built that fee price into their total price and the buyers would never even know.

Another major way that Amazon makes its money is through the use of advertisements. People who are selling their goods on Amazon are able to advertise their goods on the front page of the site and appear like they are the most popular. They must pay Amazon to be able to do this, and this is, yet another, way that Amazon is able to make money off of the people who are selling their products on the marketplace. There are some categories that are restricted from being on the front page of the Amazon website.

Most notably, Amazon is able to make money by being a retailer. Much like other companies that sell products in a retail environment, they purchase the products at a wholesale price, store them in warehouses and sell them at a markup to their clients. They do this with both "regular" products that come from other brands and their own branded products. This part of their business has proven to be the most lucrative, and it has allowed them the chance to make sure that they are truly profiting. The sale of their own products and services has made a huge impact in the way that they make money, too. Things like Kindle Unlimited, Amazon Prime, Alexa and now Echo have been able to make Amazon their own brand. A huge portion of their profits come from each of these items.

Despite the fact that Amazon is huge and they are still a retail store, their main focus is their customers. They want to make sure that their customers are always happy by offering them all of the products and services that they need. They work hard to do different things than other retailers and to offer a premium experience that people may not be able to find anywhere else on the web or even in a brick and mortar store. Amazon cares about their customers.

The fact that they care truly shows with the way that they can do different things for their clients. They know that they will be able to make sure that their clients are happy with what they have to offer. The new Amazon Echo is just one more option for their customers. It will be the ultimate customer service, tool, though because it allows customers to do everything from ordering more necessities to looking up their favorite song on the music store.

Chapter 2: Understanding this Book

This book was designed so that you would be able to better understand the way that your Amazon Echo works. It is a book that was designed for you to be able to learn as much as possible about the Echo and the way that you can use it on a daily basis. Following the advice of this book will allow you the chance to make sure that you are getting the most out of your Echo and that you will be able to do as much as possible with it when you are in different situations.

Using It

To use the book, you should first read through each of the chapters. Go in the order that they are set up so that you will be able to learn as much as possible about even the little things that Echo has to offer. The book was designed with you in mind, and it is a good idea to always follow the direction that the book is going. This will allow you the chance to learn as much as you can about the Echo.

If you skip through chapters the first time that you read the book, you may not learn everything that you can. You may skip a chapter that has important information, and it may cause you to lose out on some of the information that you could be learning about your Echo. You may also be more easily confused by some of the information that is included in the more advanced chapters. Learn the basics first, even if they seem to be boring. After you have learned the basics in the first few chapters, move on to the rest of the information about your Amazon Echo.

The Chapters

The chapters are set up in a way that they will be able to walk you through the different things that Echo can do. There are many options when it comes to Echo, and you should learn all of them so that you will be able to get the most benefit out of it. Making sure that you can do everything that you want on your Echo will give you the options that you need when it comes to what you have in your Echo device. It is important to make sure that you follow the chapters in the order that they are designed in.

The chapters, while they are each laid out in a pattern starting from the basics to the very advanced, are also laid out individually. The information that is contained in each of the chapters is designed to show you what you will be able to do and what your Echo is capable of when you are looking for different things. Make sure that you read the information contained in the chapters and that you are able to make sure that the information is all included with your Echo. Following each of the chapters will teach you a lot about your Echo.

Amazon Echo

The Amazon Echo is a tool that can be used in many different situations. You can use it when you are in your home to help you find information about a television show, about the weather and even about the different music that you want to listen to or are listening to. Amazon Echo is like having a personal assistant right in your home that is able to help you with everything that you need and does not come with the high expenses that most assistants would come from.

The only thing you need in your home to make your Amazon Echo work is wifi and who doesn't have that? The device needs wifi to be able to connect to the cloud, find information for you and get everything that you need to be able to get started with using it. It is a great device, but without the Internet, it will not be able to provide you with anything that it has to offer. There are many options for the Echo, and you should learn how to use each and every one of them through the use of it on your wireless network. There are options for different things on your Echo, and you should use the Internet to make it work.

Making it Work

The book will give you all of the information that you need to make your Echo work and to get the most out of it. The book has all of the extras about Echo that could have taken you a very long time to be able to learn if you were doing it all on your own. With the help of the book, you can learn all of your tips and tricks very easily. It will allow you the chance to learn as much as possible about the Echo in only a short amount of time.

For the book to work, you need to actually read it. While we have established that you should go through each of the chapters in the order in which they are laid out, you should also make sure that you are reading the chapters. It is not a good idea to skim through the chapters because you will not be able to learn as much as possible about the book. You will also miss out on some of the things that concern the book and the Echo, so you want to make sure that you are actually reading the chapters that have been put together.

Returning to It

Once you have read the book one time, you can then use it as a reference. You can learn what you need to learn about the different things that the book has to offer and the different things that your Echo has to offer. With the use of the book, you can always return to all of the information that you want to get started with your Echo. There are many different options for the Echo so you should always make sure that you are following the advice of the book.

Since the chapters are organized in a way that allows different information to be contained in each, you can choose which chapters you return to while you are looking for information. Since you have already read the book one time, it will be easy for you to go back and find the information for reference. This will allow you the chance to use the book any time that you want. If you have any questions about your Echo, you can return to the book for the information that you are looking for.

Chapter 3: What is Amazon Echo?

Amazon Echo is the perfect device that you never knew that you needed in your home. It is innovative and provides you with all of the resources that you need so that you will not have to worry about ever having to use your hands to find something that you need again. While it *is* all of this, there are a few other things that Amazon Echo is able to do for you in your home and with your lifestyle.

Developed

It took many years for Echo to be able to be a real thing and for the Amazon company to debut it to their customers. The developers wanted to make something that functioned as the voice control on your phone without ever having to worry about picking up your phone or having it close by. Amazon knew that people needed a real solution to be able to make things better in their homes and to figure out how they could do that had them always working on the Echo. When it was in development, they knew what they wanted, but they always continued to add to it so that they would be able to make things better for the people who would eventually be using it.

The Echo is a work in progress and something that is always changing depending on the new technologies that are available for the updates to the software. It is a great tool but it is something that can become even better with the help of the developers who are responsible for its increased abilities and for the way that it was initially developed. It was a great tool when it first came out, but it is now something that is so much better.

A Speaker

At its core, the Echo is a speaker. That is all that it is. It is required to be plugged into a power source just like any other speaker, but it has one major difference from speakers of the past and even plain speakers of today. It is a smart speaker. It requires people to hook up to the Internet to be able to use it, and this is something that gives it the capability to do more than what some of the other speakers have done in the past. It is much different in that it can do so much more than simply play your music for you.

With Echo, the speaker can do anything that you tell it to do. Unlike some of the other speakers that are on the market for simply putting out sound, Echo is able to take in sound. That means that it is not only a speaker, but it is a speaker with a microphone attached to it so that you can give it commands and tell it what you want it to do. When you tell Echo what to do, it will do what you say. For example, you can tell Echo to play a song, and it will play that song for you right from Amazon.

Alexa

When you talk to your Echo, you are actually talking to Alexa. This is the virtual assistant that is behind Echo, and she is able to provide you with the information that you need. She works in the way that virtual assistants on smartphones work, and she gives the responses based on the hardware information and the programming that she is hooked up to. Alexa has been programmed to be able to give many different responses based on the true answers. She has also been programmed to be able to continuously update to different things.

If you want to get the attention of your Echo device, all you have to do is say, Alexa. This will allow the device to turn on and will prompt it to start "listening" to your commands. You can hook up different appliances and projects in your home to be connected with your Echo. One of the most popular things that you can do is tell Alexa to turn your lights on or off in your home although that does require you to have a smart home system set up and connected to your network.

Responses

There are many different responses that Alexa may have for you. She can tell you the weather, can play your favorite song and can even help you to find something that you are looking for on Amazon while giving you the price. If you have a credit card attached to your Amazon account, she can even order that product from you by simply asking you and you responding that you want it to be ordered through your Amazon account. It is a great option for people who want to go completely hands-free.

You can put your Echo nearly anywhere in your home, and Alexa will be able to hear you. If you have more than one story in your home, though, you may want to consider two different Echo devices. This is because the hearing range of Echo *can* be limited by the different levels of division in your home. For example, you may not be able to talk to your Echo that is on the first floor if you are on the second floor because of the way that the floors are set up in your home.

Smart

Echo was designed to be a smart device. This means that Echo will learn your questions and the appropriate responses to them when you ask them to the device. You should learn to do different things with the device so that it will be able to better assist you. The more that you use your Echo, the better it will be at guessing what you are going to ask you and giving you the exact response that you are looking for whether it is a song, a movie or even what the weather is. This will give you the chance to make better use of your Echo and the way that it works for you.

As the Echo becomes more advanced, the developers continue to work on updating it. Like any other device that you have, there will be updates that you will need to be able to do to your Echo. These updates are intended to increase the number of features that you Echo has, make it run more smoothly and even allow you the chance to do more with the device than what you did in the past with it. Make sure that you always do the updates to your Amazon Echo for the best experience possible.

Chapter 4: Why Choose Echo?

There are several different devices that are available that are similar to Echo and can provide you with services that are the ones that Alexa has, but nothing is as innovative as Echo and what it promises to do for its users. It is a great option for people who want to be able to do different things but what makes it so special that you should choose it above other devices that do the same thing? Why would you want to use an Echo when you have similar services on your smartphone?

The First

Amazon Echo was the first of its type. This meant that Amazon was the one to come up with the idea for the Echo and for the tabletop smart speaker in general. The company worked hard to make sure that they were providing people with the options that they needed and they wanted to be able to use when they were at home and wanted the handsfree convenience that comes with a speaker like that.

Since Amazon was the first to be able to do this, they have been doing it for the longest. They have worked hard to make sure that even though they were the first that they always

stay as relevant as possible. It is something that allows them the chance to do more with their Echo and gives the option to do more when it comes to different things. There are many different options for Echo, and it comes from Amazon being able to work on it since they first started out.

More Options

Echo has more options than any of the other smart devices that are available for use inside your home. It is completely customizable and gives you options that some of the other devices can only hope to have in the future. Since Amazon Echo was the first, the developers have worked to make sure that they are providing their clients with the best of the best and with the most options possible. If you are hoping to have more options for your smart device and in your smart speaker, the Amazon Echo is ideal for you. It is something that will give you exactly what you want for your home and with the options that it has.

No other device gives you the ability to play your favorite song, find out the weather and shop for some of your household needs all in the same device. The Amazon Echo is the only one that does that and will continue to be one of the only ones. One special feature that nearly no other device will have in the future is the ability to read books to you. This is because Amazon owns Audible, a company that has a

books-on-tape type of feel that is made for the technology-driven world. You can *listen* to books right from your Echo.

Connected to Amazon

Another thing that most smart speakers don't have is a direct connection to the largest retailer in the world. This is because Echo is the only one that is designed to work with Amazon and because it is exclusive to the company it will be able to provide people with access to millions of different things that they can purchase. For example, you can tell Echo to send you your favorite detergent. The device will find the detergent you use the most, add it to your cart, process your payment method and send the detergent right to your home. You can even get it the next day if you have a Prime membership.

The convenience that comes with being connected to Amazon is something that no other company will ever be able to create with their smart speakers. That is because Amazon is only ever going to be able to work with the Echo. This is something that Amazon did when they were working on their Echo design so that they would be able to be exclusive. There are many things that Amazon has that no other retailer even has the ability to sell on their website.

Faster than a Phone

There have probably been countless times when you wanted to use the smart voice control on your smartphone, but you just had to keep waiting for it to continue spinning and finding exactly what you wanted it to find. This is because your phone is intended for many purposes. This can slow down the voice control feature and can make it harder for you to be able to use. This is something that is common in phones and something that has always been a problem because they can help you find things but they can be really slow about it depending on what you have on your phone.

Your Echo, on the other hand, was designed specifically for finding information for you. It is used only for that, and that gives it the chance to be able to move faster. It is a faster device and something that will always be able to find more than your smartphone. This is because it is intended to be a search engine and does not have to give some of its power to making phone calls and receiving texts. Since it is always connected to your wifi, it will only ever be as fast as your wifi allows it to be.

Less Expensive

While the Echo does boast the most features, it is surprisingly the least expensive out of many of the smart speakers that are available. You can purchase it only from

Amazon which gives them the right to price it however they want. Since there was not a lot of competition for a smart speaker when they first had the Echo, they priced it relatively low. This price has stuck and has drawn in many more customers than some of the more expensive counterparts that are available on the market. Even though Echo is the best, it is still the least expensive smart speaker.

If you are looking for something that will be able to do it all but something that will not cost you a huge amount of money, the Amazon Echo is for you. It is less expensive, gives you a huge range of capabilities and will be the best smart speaker investment that you can make.

To top it all off, it is backed by the excellent customer support that Amazon has exhibited throughout their time in business for all of the customers that they have had in that time.

Chapter 5: Setting Up Your Amazon Echo

Out of the Box

The first thing that you need to do is figure out where you are going to put your Echo. This should be somewhere that is central in your home. Many people choose to put it in the kitchen, the living room or some other common area of the home where everyone will be able to use it. If your home has more than one story, place it on the level that you are most commonly on so that it will be easier for you to access it.

You should also make sure that it is close to a power source. While it does have a cord on it, the cord is not very long and could become a tripping hazard if it is laid across the floor or even a doorway. Make sure that you put it in an area that the cord will not get in the way so that you will be able to make the most use of it without having it become a nuisance in your home. There could be problems if you don't put it in the right place. You should also have it relatively close to your router so that the connection will be as strong as possible.

Application Store

Once you have found the perfect spot for your Echo, download the Alexa app. This is where you will be able to control your Echo from and where you will be able to get the most use of it from. It is the place where you can change different settings and adjust it to work better in your home. Do not open the app as soon as you download it.

Plug in your Echo and wait for it to begin circling orange instead of the traditional blue that you would see on it. This indicates that it is ready to be configured. It will tell you that there is an update or that changes need to be made. This is an important feature, and you should always look out for the orange. This means that you cannot use the Echo while it is orange and you should do something to make changes when you see that it turns orange instead of the blue that it is supposed to be.

Wifi Connect

Once it is orange, open up the Wifi settings on your phone. Connect your phone to the "Amazon" wifi. This is where your Echo will be controlled from, and this is how you get it to link up with your wireless network that is already in your home. Once you can see that it is connected, you can open up the Alexa app. This is the app that you previously downloaded and that you will be able to make major changes to the Echo through. The app will show you that it will be connected to your own wireless network once you have it set up the right way. You can then reconnect your phone to your own wifi at that point.

If you take your phone off of the wifi that is provided by Echo too soon, you will not be able to set it up the right way. Wait for the prompt to change back to your own wifi so that you will not be missing out on some of the features that come with Echo and so that you will be able to actually use the app that comes with it. This is something that has been designed for you to make more.

Setting Up on App

From the Alexa app, you can set up everything that you need to do to make sure that your Echo is set up the right way. You will need Prime to be able to use Echo, and if you purchased your Echo through your own Prime account, you wouldn't have to worry about changing any of the settings. It will be connected, and you will be able to access all of the features from the Prime account. This is a great option and essentially allows you to plug into the electricity and go along with the app and with the way that the Echo was set up to work properly.

If you have received the Echo as a present or it is somehow not connected to your Prime account, you will need to use the "set up new device" feature on the app. This will give you the chance to manually set the settings of your Echo and connect it to your own Amazon Prime account. It will be the best option for you and will offer you the best experience possible for your Alexa and for Echo. There are many options that you can choose when you make the decision to use this feature.

Alexa

The Echo was designed to respond to "Alexa." When you say the word "Alexa," it will start to listen to what you are saying. If you want to search for something that is on your Amazon, you can say, "Alexa, find the Bon Jovi song that I listened to 4 times yesterday." Alexa will work to find that song through your Prime account and will give you the chance to listen to the song. This is something that you can do no matter what you are looking for. You must use Alexa.

There will be times when Alexa will carry on and give you information that you don't really need to know. This can also be triggered if a child says it or is searching for something that is inappropriate. All you need to say is: "Alexa, stop."

When you say that, the Echo will stop talking, and you will be able to start over with what you really wanted to be able to search for instead of listening to it carry on in the drone that it can sometimes have.

The real problem comes when someone in your house is named Alexa! But, that's not really a problem. If you have someone in your house named Alexa or if you simply don't want to use the name, you can change it through the app to respond to "Amazon." All you have to say is "Hey, Amazon" in the same way that you would use the Alexa watchword.

Chapter 6: Compatible Echo Apps

There are many different ways that Amazon Echo can work well for you on its own, but you can make it even better by using some of the compatible apps with it. These apps include things that you can add on as well as things that can make everything even better. While you can get the weather, information and everything else that you need on your own with Echo, you can also use other apps to make it truly a phenomenal tool.

Spelling Bee

One of the many features that come with Echo is games. You can play a variety of different games that come in different categories. One of the most popular is a spelling bee: all you have to do is ask Alexa to play the spelling bee, and you can go head to head with your best friends on the game.

Batman Adventure

If you are more interested in a game that you can choose your own outcome with, the Batman adventure is something that is probably more your speed. The game allows you to do many different things and to make different choices with the game. As you choose different things, you can figure out different outcomes. The game is different each time that you play it so that you will never get board.

Jeopardy

With a twist on the classic game, you can go up to your friends and family members to learn who is the best and who knows the most. This game is fun for everyone to play and is a real party starter. Simply ask Alexa to play Jeopardy! She'll be there. There are many different ways that you can play the game so make sure you have Alexa give you plenty of options. This game can simply be added to your Alexa app and can be hooked up to it. It does not require a second app to purchase or to download to be able to play this game. It is built into Alexa and can simply be selected from the Alexa app on your phone.

Automatic

If your car has a smart device or does have the smart device feature already included in it, you can use your Alexa to make it even better. Take automatic start by letting Alexa know that you want your car to start before you even get out of bed in the morning. This is a great way to save time. You can also look at the health of your car and decide whether or not you need to change the oil or add fluids to it depending on what is going on with the car at that time.

Capital One

If you need to manage all of these apps that you're paying for along with all of your other bills, Echo has you covered on that front, too. You can use the Capital One app and hook it up to your Echo device so that you are able to make sure that you pay your bill on time. You can even use it to check your balance, see your transaction history and add on authorizations to the account. In the future, Capital One promises that you will be able to transfer your money from Echo to someone else using the Capital One app hooked up to Alexa.

News

Echo is so much better than reading the Sunday morning paper. All you need to do is ask Alexa to show you the news, and she will give you a rundown of everything that went on through the day. If you ask her in the morning, she'll catch you up on everything that you missed last night and the day before. This feature does not require you to download anything extra and is included with Alexa for the best features possible when it comes to the news.

Dominos

Feeling like you want to order in but don't want to have to go through all of the trouble? Create a profile with Dominos including your credit card information and hook the

Dominos app up to your Alexa. It is easy, all you need to do is have both of the apps on your phone to be able to use it. This will be a great option. You can let Alexa know to order your favorite order, which you can save in your Dominos app. You can also create custom orders, hear the menu or ask Alexa to tell you what is on special for the week at Dominos.

Quick Events

If you want to hear the news, but just don't have the time to listen to it all, you can tell Alexa to list the quick events. This gives you a simple rundown of everything that is going on and is just a recap of the recent events that went on throughout the day. Alexa will give you snippets and will let you know the important things. If you are particularly interested in things, like the stock market, you can change your settings and prioritize your quick events through the app. You can also just listen to all of the things that *could* be important.

Working Out

Echo does it all! Amazon has come up with 7-minute workouts that you can do right with your Echo device. Tell Alexa to find you 7-minute high-intensity interval training, and she will get you exactly what you need. This is perfect for people who are on the go, people who like to do more with their mornings and people who just want to be able to get the best workout possible in the shortest amount of time. There are many different options you can choose from the app, but there is no need for a different special app to use this.

Uber

Anyone who is running late for their flight can know how critical time is. There is an easy way to cut down on time. Connect your Alexa app to your Uber app and get ready to go. All you have to do is summon Alexa and ask her to call you an Uber. There will be one there in no time. You can even let her know what your preferences are for the premium and different options that come with the Uber app. You can also present this in your Uber app, so you never have to specify.

Chapter 7: Amazon Prime Music

Along with everything else that Amazon Prime has, they also have music that can be used with the Alexa application. There are many different music streaming services that are available on the Internet, but Echo only uses the Amazon Music because it is, of course, connected to your Amazon account. While this may be disappointing for some Pandora or iHeart users, there are countless benefits that users can get from Amazon Music that they would never have a chance to use with any other online radio.

Amazon vs. Tune In

When you listen to Amazon music, you get all of the songs at the touch of your fingertips. Much like the Kindle Unlimited application that you can get from Amazon, you can also get the music that you want to listen to any time that you want to listen to it. All of the songs that you could get from Amazon Music are included with your Prime membership so that you don't have to worry about any extra add-ons.

With Tune In radio, you can add it to your Kindle or other Amazon device. You can also add it to Alexa. The problem with this is that you have to listen to it in the same way that you would listen to traditional radio. You listen to what comes on, and you cannot pick and choose to customize the stations. This is, perhaps, one of the least popular competitors of Amazon music. While it is sold by Amazon and falls under their licensing, it is far inferior to everything that Amazon Music has to offer the people who listen to it.

The clear winner is Amazon Music because of everything that it has to offer. You can listen to any song that you would like at anytime and anywhere. With the Echo, you can also just listen to your favorite songs by speaking about what you want. "Alexa, play "Don't Stop Believin'.""

Amazon vs. iHeart Radio

iHeart Radio is one of the more popular radio options available for people who want to listen to an actual radio service on the Internet. You can enjoy everything from talk radio to sports to any of the music that you would like but, again, you cannot listen to it in the on-demand format that you get from Amazon Music. The radio that is provided by iHeart Radio is great for people who want to listen to something that is mixed up and random but is not great for people who want to be able to actually choose the songs that they are going to listen to.

Amazon music is able to provide you everything that you would get with the iHeart radio without all of the randomnesses. You can choose to use the application that is included with your Echo to listen to everything that you would like, including talk shows and sports. Amazon Music has something for everyone, and you will be able to find it right there.

While iHeart Radio is an available app that you can use with Alexa, it may be something that you don't necessarily need. Amazon Music is a much better choice, is free with your Amazon Prime membership and can be customized to suit your needs. The only thing that Amazon Music does not have that iHeart Radio *does* have is the ability to play music based on the mood that you are in or the way that you feel like listening to music.

Amazon vs. Pandora

As one of the most popular music streaming services, Pandora is one of the biggest competitors when it comes to Amazon Music. This is because of the way that it is used to be able to help people listen to their favorite music based on artists, moods, and genres. Pandora has been on the scene for a very long time, and the chances of them going away anytime soon are very slim. Many people use Pandora on their phones, on their computer and even in the car so that they are able to listen to their favorite music. Pandora, still, though, is only a streaming service.

As with all of the other streaming and radio services that Amazon Music has come up against, they are able to beat out Pandora with the fact that they can play customized tunes for you to be able to listen to. While your Amazon Music subscription is included with your Amazon Prime membership, you would have to pay Pandora even more money to be able to listen to their premium version. The only problem with that is that their premium version does not even include the ability to listen to specific songs. It just eliminates commercials and allows you to skip through the radio playback.

While Pandora has been one of the biggest radio competitors on the Internet scene, it is still just a radio service. Amazon Music has been able to beat all of these other ones out because they just stream music and Amazon give you access to *choose* your music, but will they be able to beat out their most similar rival?

Amazon vs. Spotify

After the three-month Spotify 99 cent trial, users are expected to pay $10 per month for the service. That is a $120 cost to people just to be able to listen to the radio and choose the music that they want to be able to play. It is an application for you to be able to listen to music in the radio format for free but if you want to be able to listen to songs, you need to get the premium version.

With Amazon Music, you get it included with your Amazon Prime account. This means that you only have to pay the Prime fee – $99 per year – to be able to enjoy all of the benefits of the Amazon Music. This is a $21 savings for you and you not only get the Amazon Music, but you get all of the other features that are included with Prime. It is a great option for you to be able to choose Amazon Music for your Amazon Prime subscription.

With the savings comes along many other benefits that Spotify doesn't offer. Amazon Music has the option to allow you to listen to many different music choices. Spotify, on the other hand, does not have quite as many artists as what Amazon Music has. This is because they lost many of their agreements with some recording artists. Amazon Music is still able to keep those agreements up.

Overall, Amazon Music is a great choice for anyone who wants to be able to stream music and listen to the music that they want. It offers many different options and the flexibility to be able to listen to nearly anything that you want. On top of all of the other amazing benefits that come with using your Amazon Music that is included in your Prime Membership is the fact that you can use it already integrated into with your Echo. All you need to do is tell Alexa to play your favorite songs!

Chapter 8: Design and Setup of Alexa

Alexa has been working for you for the entire time that the Amazon Echo has been available on the market. The computer generated Alexa has been able to find different things, work with different applications and enable you to have the easiest experience possible. While it was not the first smart computer programming, it is one of the best that is available. It is also one of the only ones that are not built into a phone and can only be used with a phone (we see you, Siri).

Setup of Alexa

Alexa is truly easy for you to be able to setup. The program comes preinstalled on your Echo device, and there is not much that you need to do to be able to use it. Once you have done the initial setup, you can really just go with it. The Alexa program will be able to do the majority of the work.

The most important part about Alexa is that your Echo is connected to the same Wifi that your phone (and the Alexa app) is connected to. It is important that you keep your Echo on a wireless network all of the time so that it will be able to actually work.

Without the wireless network, you will not be able to use your Echo. This is because it runs off of wifi just like many of your other smart devices do. Make sure that you do everything that you can to keep your Echo up to date and always use the fastest Internet speed available so that you can get the most out of your Echo. The faster that you have when it comes to the Internet, the better your Echo will be able to perform.

The Alexa App

The Alexa app is able to be downloaded on any app store. It can be used with any phone or tablet, but it works better if you have Wifi. The app is able to let you do the initial setup of your Echo device. After that, you never have to use the app again but doing so will allow you to truly customize your experience with your Echo. Make sure that you are getting the most out of it with the Alexa app. You can even change the watchword to something that is more suitable for your household.

Always make sure that your Alexa app is up to date. The app store will give you different updates for it, and you must do them to make sure that Alexa is giving you all of the features that it has. Do the updates and keep up with the app so that you can make sure you are getting everything that you need out of Echo. You never know when you'll miss an important update. It could even include the ability to buy more carryout right from your Echo device.

It Gets Smarter

When you use your Echo more, it learns more about you. This is especially true when it comes to music and books. The Alexa software will begin to look for things that you enjoy and will give you the chance to see that you are going to pick something even better than what it picked the last time. Make sure that you are prepared for this and that you are using your Echo whenever possible. The more you use it, the better it will be able to work for you.

Since Alexa has bene programmed for you and is able to increase its abilities the more that it learns about you, you should make sure that you are using it. Even the app is something that will learn your preferences quickly. Amazon has come up with this to make life easier and to make things better for you. The Echo is intended to be a great device that will be able to give you exactly what you want when it comes to the different options that you have. Whether you want to listen to music, play an audiobook or learn what traffic is going to be like on Route 70, you'll be able to get everything that you need from Echo.

Designed for You

The Echo device and the Alexa programming is designed for people. Amazon is all about the customer experience, and it is something that will make things better for people. Your Alexa has been designed with you in mind. The app, like the device, is customizable to your preferences. You can make sure that you are getting the most out of both by always using them whenever you can.

The customer experience with Echo is great. Amazon is all about customer service, and that is no different with Echo. You can make sure that you are provided the best by always doing your best. Amazon Echo can be used, and there could be many different things that you can do. Even if you have a problem with your Amazon Echo, you will be able to get a great customer experience out of it through the use of Amazon. Always make sure that you are doing the best job possible and that the company will work together with you to make things even better.

All Information

All of the information that Alexa has comes from a huge database that was created by Amazon. This includes the news that comes directly from actual news sources, the music that comes from Amazon's vast collection and the capabilities of some of the best search engines around. When you use Alexa, you will know that you are getting all of the best information on the web. You can find out everything that you need to know and you will be able to get a great deal out of everything that you have. There are so many options that Alexa has, and you will be surprised.

Make sure that you use your Echo so that you can get the most out of the vast information that is included in the design of the Echo and the setup of the Alexa service.

Chapter 9: Practical Applications of Alexa

While Alexa is a great thing to have for entertainment and fun, there are also many practical applications of the Echo device and everything that comes along with it. Not only will you be able to play fun games or order pizza, but there are other things that Alexa can help you with when it comes to your day-to-day routine in your home. These practical uses are perfect for anyone who wants to save some time.

Home Control

If you have any type of smart device in your home, Alexa is able to hook up to it. This means that you can turn your lights on from a different room, can raise the garage door and even unlock the front door for your parents who are coming over to visit while you are cooking.

If you have smart lights, you can change the color of them just by asking Alexa to do so. If you have multiple Echo devices or dots in your home, you can use Alexa to change the lights or even the music in one room to a different room.

When it comes to the different things that Alexa can do in your home, the limits are only as far as the smart devices that you have. Alexa is able to hook up with nearly any smart device, and this can change the way that you do things in your home. Make sure that you are able to get the most out of the experience with Alexa by getting all of the best smart devices in your home and with the different options that your Echo has.

To-Do Lists

How many times have you thought about something but forgot about it before you had a chance to write it down on your to-do list? The chances are that happens a lot, and you may not know what to do with yourself when it *does* happen. Now, with Echo, you can just ask Alexa to add it to your to-do list. Alexa will keep a running tally of all of the things that you want to put on there, and she will remember what you told her you wanted to add onto it. All you have to do to get your to-do list is ask Alexa for it.

With all of the new innovations and updates, your Echo can now handle multiple to-do lists. You may want to set up one for your home office, one for your home and one for errands that you need to run later on in the day. No matter what you want to be able to do, you should consider making different to do lists for Alexa so that she will be able to help you out with the different things that you need to get done.

Traffic

Traffic can take up a huge chunk of your day. Whether you are traveling to work, to the grocery store or to the airport, you need to have a good idea of what the traffic will be like. You can ask Alexa for a specific route to figure out the traffic, or you can just ask about traffic in your city in general. Alexa will give you all of the information that you need on the traffic in your area so that you will be able to know ahead of time before you even leave the house.

While it is true that your GPS can do the same thing, it does so in real time. With Alexa, you can truly plan ahead to figure out what the traffic is going to be like in that area. It is a good idea to know before you even leave the house so that you don't have to worry about what you are going to do once you get on the road and once you know where you are going to go. Alexa is like having a GPS without ever having to leave the house.

Playlists

Even though you can make playlists on your Amazon Music account, the application can also generate playlists based on moods or events that are going to happen. For example, you can ask Alexa to play music to help you get ready to go out on the town. You can also ask her to play sad music if you are upset about a breakup or something else that is going on in your life. Make sure that you ask Alexa to play the music that you want no matter the mood that you are in.

It is also a great idea to create your own playlists. If you are listening to Amazon Music or even one of the other supported apps, like Pandora, you can tell Alexa to add a specific song to your favorite playlist. For example, if you hear something that you like, you can just tell Alexa to add this to your "favorites" music playlist. This will allow the song to be added and you can listen to it anytime that you want. This is especially handy for songs that you often hear on a music app but just don't know the name of or have the time to find out what they are all about.

Weather

The weather outside is nearly as important as finding out what the traffic is like where you are going. What are you going to wear? What do you need to bring along? Just ask Alexa. You can even ask Alexa if you need your rainboots and she'll let you know what the weather is going to be like for the day. You can do this as soon as you wake up if you keep Alexa in your bedroom with you.

You can also have this as your alarm. You can set Alexa to tell you the weather when it is time for you to get up. This essentially gives the alarm two different functions. It will wake you up to tell you that it is time to get up, but it will also tell you what you need to do to prepare for the day. Make sure that you have it set to that on your Alexa application. You cannot change it from your Echo, but you will be able to change it from the Alexa app. Be sure that your city is set in the right place so that Alexa doesn't give you the weather in Boulder if you're actually in Sacramento. You may be unpleasantly surprised with your rain boot choice that day!

Chapter 10: Tips and Tricks for Echo

Along with the more practical things that Alexa is able to do on your Amazon Echo, she can also do some really fun things. These don't have too much of a purpose although they can be useful in some situations. Try out any of these tips to get a great idea of what you can *really* do with your Amazon Echo.

Math Problems

This is one of the tips that is fun and has a practical application. Alexa is so complex that she is able to do most math problems that you ask her. While she might not necessarily be up for the challenge of advanced statistics or any other type of advanced math courses, you can ask her simple math questions.

You can use your Echo as a homework helper, a way to figure something out quickly or to even find out what type of measurements you should be using while you are making a recipe. Alexa is able to quickly and easily convert your measurements into exactly what you need to be able to use.

Repeat It

Sometimes, Alexa will begin to talk very fast, and you may have a hard time keeping up with what she is saying or the way that she is saying it. You can combat this by making sure that you know the commands to get her to repeat it. You can't just say "REPEAT" at your Echo device, but you can say,

"Alexa, can you slow down," or,

"Alexa, could you say that again?"

Each of these commands will cause Alexa to talk more slowly and repeat exactly what she said the first time for you to be able to hear.

Something for Everyone

The Echo comes with options for different family members. Each person can have a personality on the Echo, and it will be tailored to the features that they like to use. In the past, you needed to be able to use the app to change this and set it up, but you can now use the actual Echo device to be able to set it up since there are many different features available. All you have to do is ask your Echo to switch between the different profiles that you have made on your Echo. No need for the app!

Voice Remote

There are different accessories that you can use with your Echo. One of these is the Amazon voice remote. If you don't want to always use your Echo in the room that you are in, the voice remote will work well for you to be able to use. You can tell your Echo what you want to be able to do and let it know the commands that you have for it right from the remote. The remote works in the same way as you would be able to talk to your Echo. This is something that is new to the Echo and will work seamlessly with the Alexa app.

Track Shipping

Anything that you have purchased from Amazon is able to be tracked from the Amazon website. You can also use Echo to be able to track this information. All you need to ask is for Alexa to track the shipping on your purchase. If you have several different purchases that you have made through Prime, she will ask you to clarify which one. This will be done with an order number or with the items that were to help you have a better idea of what the package shipment is.

Flip a Coin

Anyone who has had a hard time deciding what they want to eat for dinner will be able to appreciate the flip a coined feature that is provided by the Echo device. All you need to do is decide whether you are heads or tails and then ask Echo to flip a coin for you. This doesn't only need to be done for dinner – it can also be done with major decisions that you just can't seem to come to an agreement on.

Exclusive Deals

People who own the Echo device will have access to exclusive deals to Amazon. Along with the deals that you get from the traditional Amazon Prime experience, having an Echo will also give you the chance to be able to get even more deals. Make sure that you connect your Echo with your Prime membership or simply purchase your Echo through your Prime account so that you will be able to get the deals as soon as possible. You may be surprised to find you are able to get the most out of it when you are making sure that you get the full experience. You can also get exclusive items that are only available for people who have an Echo.

Santa

Even inquiring minds will be able to enjoy the benefits of Echo. You need to make sure that you are getting the most out of the experience and so do your kids. Since Alexa knows that kids will sometimes be around the device, she is prepared with all of the answers. For example, if your child wants to know whether or not Santa is real, Echo will not give them an answer. Instead, Alexa will just tell your child that Santa is a great man that she has heard of. While Alexa isn't completely kid-proof, yet, there are some safeguards that are in there for kids to be able to make sure that things are still innocent and naïve.

Celebrities

When Echo was first available, there were several celebrities who did the commercials. These celebrities (and their respective voices) can now be found right in your Echo device. For example, asking certain questions about a certain Baldwin brother will give you the ability to learn a little about him and to hear everything that he has to say in his own voice. Get a little bit of celebrity love.

Whether you are using your Echo to settle a dispute, learn about a math question or even find out more about the big guy in red, you will be able to get the most out of the situation. It is a good idea to make sure that you set up family profiles so that different people in your family will be able to get exactly what they need from experience. There are many different options available to you, and you should take advantage of nearly all of the tips that are available for you to use on your Amazon Echo device.

Chapter 11: More to Come

Amazon is so much more than a typical retailer. They have something for everyone, and they are constantly coming up with new ideas for you to be able to purchase. The new items that are coming from Amazon are great for everyone from people who love technology to people who just need to have an easier time in their daily lives. There are many options to choose from, and the upcoming books will have more information about each of these products. Stay tuned for more to come but be sure to read on for a little glimpse into what each product will have for you to be able to use.

Echo Dot

If you want to get all of the features of the Echo without the price that comes with the Echo, you can benefit from the Echo Dot. In essence, the Dot is just the top of the Echo. It only has one speaker and will not be able to project sound from many different areas. This is meant for you to use with your own speakers or your own system in your home. You can even hook it up with your surround sound.

The Dot does not sacrifice on anything other than price, sound, and size. It has all of the same features that the Echo does. This is a great product for people who live in small apartments, people who want to use an Echo but don't want to make a huge commitment and people who already have a smart home system set up that they can integrate the Dot into so that they will have one more feature and so that they can control it with their voice. Many people choose to use the Dot so that they can have several Echos throughout their house.

Tablets

Slightly different from the original reader that Amazon came out with, the tablets offer everything that you would expect from a tablet in today's technology-driven world. The tablets that are created by Amazon are able to provide you with the experience that you need from the tablet and the support that you have likely come to expect from Amazon. Make sure that you use the tablet in any way that you would typically use a tablet. It is a good idea to make sure that you have wifi.

Some of the tablets that come from Amazon are able to be used on 3G, but you need to have that service to be able to use them. Be sure that you are getting exactly what you want by checking to see if your service will support the tablet. Make sure that you learn as much as possible about the tablet and that you can get a great experience out of it. If you are looking for something different, consider a Fire tablet.

Amazon also makes a tablet that is exclusive for kids. It is safer than the adult ones and has fewer features so that your kids do not get overwhelmed with the options on their tablets.

Fire TV

Amazon's Fire TV gives you all of the streaming options that you never knew that you needed but that you can now have at your fingertips. You can connect your Prime Account with the Fire TV so that you will be able to listen to and watch all of your favorite shows right from the comfort of your home. You don't need to worry about anything that comes along with it because Prime has made everything a reality for you when it comes to Fire TV.

Even if you are not accustomed to using Fire TV, there are many options that you can include with the Prime membership that you have. You can make sure that you get the most out of them by reading about it in the upcoming book and doing everything that you have learned from it with the TV. You may be surprised at some of the tips that can tell you things that you need to do and things that you can add on to the TV to make sure that you get the most out of it and that you are doing the best job possible with the TV.

SmartHome

Your Echo will be so much more valuable if you have the Smart Home products in your home that you can use to make things easier for you. There are many options that the Echo has that allow you to connect things together and to make sure that you are getting the most out of the experience.

When it comes to the Home products, there are countless things that you can do and that you can add onto. The new book with all of this information will give you the insight that you need to be able to use them the right way. Make sure that you read all about it so that you can get the most out of it and so that you are getting the best experience possible when it comes to both your Echo and your Smart Home products. You can use everything from doorknobs to light switches and everything in between. Your home can be as efficient as possible, and you can learn all about it in the new book.

Kindles

As one of Amazon's first technology products, the Kindle has come such a long way. In the past, it was a tablet and a reader in one, but it has grown to be so much more. When it split off with the Fire tablets, it was able to focus solely on the reader capabilities. As one of the first on the market, Amazon has been able to make their reader the best for people who want to get a true reading experience out of their eBooks. The reader is compatible with both Amazon Prime and Kindle Unlimited. It is mainly for reading, but it does have a few other features that people can enjoy when they are using the reader.

One of the best features that are included with your Kindle is paperwhite. This allows the screen to have no glare on it in the way that a traditional tablet screen would. This allows you to read even on the sunniest of days and in the most nontraditional places. Reading on the beach is a completely new experience when you have the paperwhite view to check out with your Kindle.

To learn more about the Kindle and everything that you can do with it along with some of the best books for it, be sure to check out the Kindle book. You could even get a Kindle specifically to read the Kindle book. That way, you could practice while you are reading about it which makes the experience so much better.

With everything that Amazon has to offer in its product lineup, there is a product for everyone. Whether you are a movie buff, someone who loves to read or you simply crave simplicity in your life, you can get what you need from Amazon products. The upcoming books will be able to tell you everything that you need to know about each of the products. Each of the products will have their own information, and you can learn a lot from what the books will have to offer you.

Conclusion

Thank for making it through to the end of this book, let's hope it was informative and able to provide you with all of the tools you need to achieve your goals whatever they may be.

The next step is to go get your Echo and try out everything that you have learned in each of the chapters of the book.

Finally, if you found this book useful in any way, a review on Amazon is always appreciated!

Description

If you have an Amazon Echo or are thinking about getting an Echo, this is the book for you. The book will teach you everything that you need to know about the Echo and what it can do for you. There are many different tips and tricks that you probably have never heard of in this book.

The book is organized in a way that will be easy for you to understand. All of the information is split up and easy to navigate. Each of the chapters focuses on a different area, and you can use this to make your experience better. It gives you all of the information that you need for the Amazon Echo.

Make sure that you follow along with the book. It will take you from the setup to using it for practical applications and even some of the fun things that you can do with the Echo. There may even be some hidden tips in with the book so that you can do cool things nobody else knows how to do on their Echo.

If you have already purchased and set up your Amazon Echo, you can make sure that you are getting the most out of your

product. The book will give you all of the advice that you need to make your Echo device better and will be one of the best investments that you can make for your Echo so that you can learn as much about it as possible. When it comes to the Echo, you will be able to get the most use out of it if you know everything that you can do with it.

Even if you have not purchased an Echo and are just thinking about getting one, you can still benefit from the book. It will give you a glimpse of what you can do with the Echo and how it can help you out in your daily life. It will make you better prepared to get your Echo and to use it in the most efficient way possible when you do purchase it.

Read on for more information about the Echo and how it can improve your life!